Teach Your Preschooler to Read & Write

By John Bowman

Teach Your Preschooler to Read & Write

ISBN #: 978-0-9891768-7-3

Cover Photo: *Shutterstock*

An eBook edition is available in the Kindle Store on Amazon.

The information presented here is for parents to use according to their time, interest, and capabilities. Not all parents will see the same results using the activities shown here. No guarantees are made or implied. Success with early learning activities requires the right approach to encourage a child's interest and enthusiasm, and consistency over time. Reading and writing skills develop in a sequence; following it gives the best results.

The author receives no compensation or other benefit from the providers of materials, apps, and other resources recommended in this book. All are included on the basis of their quality and value for parents.

When working with young children, **keep safety in mind first**. Children under three should not use small objects that could cause choking. If the object rolls easily through a toilet paper roll, it is too small for three year olds and younger. Look for sharp points and edges and be sure your child handles learning materials carefully. Remove any materials that pose a hazard to a child or that a child is not able to use safely.

Table of Contents

More books by the author

Montessori At Home!

www.montessoriathomebook.com

The Third Edition (2013, $10.95) is a 576-page pdf eBook guide to doing an entire Montessori preschool program at home. Complete Montessori how-to information for parents, over 300 activities in Practical Life, Sensorial, Art & Music, Digital Life, Science, Mathematics, Writing, and Reading, hundreds of links to sites, blogs, and videos to expand on the information in the eBook, an extensive collection of printables, and recommendations for over 200 of the very best educational digital tablet apps. The best value in early childhood education for parents. Purchase at the site above.

"I am more than impressed with the eBook. The integration of video, links, and photos throughout the book are amazing. I've never read anything like it! Many thanks for such a wonderful resource. I am truly impressed and grateful to have access to this guide for implementing Montessori at home."

Jeanette, Ed.S. School Psychologist

Help Your Preschooler Build a Better Brain (2013, on Amazon in Kindle and paperback editions). The Kindle eBook edition has most of the same information as the Montessori At Home! eBook, in convenient Kindle format for reading on your laptop or mobile device using the free Kindle app. The paperback is a condensed version for those preferring paper books.

"Truly excellent resource to help parents understand how a preschooler learns by discovery and exploration. A practical, easy-to-follow handbook for designing and implementing activities at home to encourage independence and early learning. Wonderful, relevant information and illustrations, web references, and recommended items help parents get started in designing their own prepared environment for their preschooler. Very well-done, step-by-step guide!"

Polarbear07

"This book is a true gem. The author offers countless ways to introduce your children to complex concepts through fun and interesting experiments. Many of the lessons are Montessori based and can be easily replicated at home. A really great find!"

Claire David

Teach Your 3-7 Year Old Math (2014, Amazon Kindle & paperback editions) gives parents a complete Montessori-style program for helping their children learn about amounts and numerals into the thousands, the decimal system, operations with numbers, fractions, geometry, and practical uses of math skills in daily life. If you want to concentrate on math, this is the eBook for you. Most of the activities here are included in the larger books above.

"What a brilliant resource with so many practical ways to teach math. John writes in such an engaging way and is so thorough. This book covers the when, what, why and how of teaching a young child math. Truly packed full of information, examples, resources and suggestions. This is worth so much more than it's selling for! I genuinely recommend this (and his other books) to every parent who wants to teach their children in an effective, practical, & affordable way."

Rachel at Loveable Learning

"Covers a vast array of math concepts with wonderful real life situations in which to learn and practice skills. Highly recommended!"

Cindy

Introduction

Over many years in our Montessori schools we helped hundreds of 3-6 year old children learn to write and read. In Montessori, skills are not pushed on children. The interest comes from the child's inner self-motivation to learn and grow. When the fire of curiosity is burning, a child can learn almost anything. We help children learn to write and read during the 3-6 age range because that is when children have a natural affinity for learning written language, not because we want to push these skills on children.

We worked out a simple approach that deviates from the classic Montessori language sequence, but which we felt fits more closely with how children today naturally develop written language skills. That sequence of materials and activities is described here. You can easily use these materials and activities at home to teach your child to read and write, without special training or great expense.

Writing comes first and easier for most children. Even using primitive hand grasps, very young children draw with chalk, crayons, and markers. As their hand and finger control improves and they move towards a proper writing grasp, they become interested in letters and words. Writing is the next step. Reading requires more complex skills. Here is how Maria Montessori described it:

"...the muscular sense is most easily developed in infancy, and this makes writing exceedingly easy for children. It is not so with reading, which requires a much longer course of instruction, and which calls for a superior intellectual development, since it treats of the interpretation of signs, and of the modulation of accents of the voice, in order that the word may be understood. And all this is a purely mental task while in writing the child....materially translates sounds into signs, and moves a thing, which is always pleasant for him. Reading...is the interpretation of ideas from graphic symbols..."

In just a few years, your preschooler has learned an incredible amount of spoken language. She knows thousands of words, can learn other languages if exposed to them regularly, communicates her needs and thoughts, knows by the sound of your voice what the same words mean when used in different ways, and can recognize irony, satire, and humor. This is an amazing accomplishment that we take for granted in children. It demonstrates that children have a skilled Inner Teacher guiding their development. Learning to write and read is simply an extension of what your child already knows about spoken language.

Writing starts with developing a proper writing grasp with the fingers, drawing and tracing, and finally learning to consistently reproduce the line symbols known as letters and numerals. Reading starts with successful experiences with learning letter sounds, building words from them, and reading simple phonetic readers. Next, your child learns to recognize words when she sees them, and combines words to make all kinds of sentences. Finally, your child starts reading simple books, gradually moving on to more challenging books. It is a simple process that makes perfect sense once you see it laid out in sequence.

Start at the beginning and give your child plenty of time to practice. Be positive, be patient, and encourage your child's efforts. Early learning should be a fun series of discoveries, challenges, mistakes, and achievements. Taking the journey with your child can be one of life's great experiences. Have fun!

Your child's spontaneously expressed interests are always your best guide for what kinds of activities to offer. With suitable activities and learning materials, you will see your child gradually learn to focus her attention and concentration for extended periods of time. This is the key to brain development in early childhood. Children who focus their attention become happier, better adjusted children. Maria Montessori called this process 'Normalization':

"Only "normalised" children, aided by their environment, show in their subsequent development those wonderful powers that we describe: spontaneous discipline, continuous and happy work, social sentiments of help and sympathy for others. . . . An interesting piece of work, freely chosen, which has the virtue of inducing concentration rather than fatigue, adds to the child's energies and mental capacities, and leads him to self-mastery. . . . One is tempted to say that the children are performing spiritual exercises, having found the path of self-perfection and of ascent to the inner heights of the soul."

Maria Montessori, *The Absorbent Mind*

Download your free printables

Type the URL below in your browser to download a free set of printable materials for use with many of the activities in this book:

tinyurl.com/q9ta2dp

Included are 8 classroom quality printables from Montessori Print Shop, which cost $6 purchased separately – thanks, MPS! Here is a list of the printables in your free set:

Montessori Print Shop Printables

Montessori Blue Triangle Three Part Cards

Color Grading Cards

Superimposed Geometric Figures

Metal Inset Shape Outlines

Animal Match Up & Memory Cards

Noun Sorting Cards

Pre-Printing Tracing Pages

Initial Sound Choice Cards

Montessori At Home! Printables

Animal Types Sorting

Fruit Sorting

Banana Size Grading

Squirrels Size Grading

Circles Grading

Geometric Solids Name Cards

Geometric Shapes Name Cards

Geometric Shapes Templates

Movable Alphabet Master Sheets

Dolch Sight Word Flash Cards

Reading and Writing are Natural

Shutterstock

Your child is genetically prepared to learn to write and read. It is appropriate to help preschool age children learn these skills, because the ages 3-6 are when we are programmed by nature to learn written language. These years are the Sensitive Period for this, and other things such as mathematics. Provide the activities and experiences described here during these years and your child will learn to read and write without pressure or stress. Any parent can do this, without headaches or spending a lot of money.

We adults make everything complicated. Learning written language is no exception. Baby Einstein, Hooked on Phonics, whole language, context support, online programs, tablet apps – the choices alone are enough to give you a migraine. Even teachers argue about it! Children don't care about all this. They just want to know what words say so they can get in on the action.

Programs like Baby Einstein and Baby Can Read are mainly good at separating well - meaning parents from their money. Child development follows a natural sequence. The infant and toddler years are not the natural time for children to learn to read and write. These are the years for acquiring verbal language skills and direct sensory impressions of the environment, not for watching television, using tablet apps, or staring at flash cards. Writing and reading become appropriate when a child enters the natural sensitive period for learning these skills, usually between 3 to 6 years of age.

By age three children have mastered an incredible amount of information about verbal language and have developed good basic verbal communication skills. Soon after this, they naturally become interested in learning to write and read.

Helping your own child develop these important life skills is a wonderful experience. It is a total joy to send your child to kindergarten or first grade already knowing how to read. This will give your child a wonderful head start that can translate into continued success throughout the school years.

Although it is seductive to start teaching a child writing and reading too early, the reason many children struggle with reading and writing in school is that they start too late. If all children had access to materials and activities for learning to read and write in the natural sensitive period from ages 3-6, they wouldn't have nearly as many problems in school later.

If your child is in kindergarten or first grade and is having trouble getting into reading or writing, the activities here can turn things around and give your child the wonderful experience of being successful at learning to read and write. The good news today is that there are more materials and activities available for early learning than ever.

"The most favorable age for the development of written language is that of childhood, about the age of four, when the natural processes connected with the development of speech are fully activated, that is, during the sensitive period when speech naturally develops and becomes fixed. A child's sensitiveness to his own development arouses his enthusiasm for learning the alphabet and urges him on to make a phonetic analysis of words into their component sounds.....That is why little children as a rule make better and more rapid progress than those who are older. Instead of becoming bored and weary like the older children, they carry on a constant activity that seems to strengthen them."

Maria Montessori

Digital Learning

Many parents and teachers, welcome tablet apps as the future of education for all children, even from the earliest years. "*Look at how much fun they have, and they are learning, too!*" It is seductively easy, however, to use tablets as convenient babysitters to keep the kids quiet. There are other folks who think young children should never be exposed to apps, computers, or anything digital. Exposing preschoolers to screens is a controversial, often emotional topic, generating strong opinions on either side.

I believe that high quality, educational tablet apps have a place in the lives of young children. The trick is when to introduce them, what apps to use, and how to structure your child's digital experiences.

The development of abstract thought

We can, and should, look to how children naturally develop for our guide. Among the many developmental achievements of young children, one stands out as perhaps the most important to consider when deciding whether and when to use educational tablet apps: the development of abstract thought.

As Maria Montessori observed, young children, from birth to around six, are in a stage of life where their most vital need is for direct sensory and neuromuscular experience with their environment. They need to handle, manipulate, smell, hear, see, and taste the world to start understanding it as more than a magic show. Little children have to move and use their bodies and experience the real world directly in order to develop their brains.

Cutting beans, Little House Montessori

Accumulating a large storehouse of direct impressions of the real world is essential for proper brain development in the first years of life. Too much screen time with TV, apps, or computers in these years gets in the way of the all-important need to experience the world directly. There is only one way to understand the world later, and that is to experience it directly first.

Sometime around four, although their need for direct sensory experience remains high, most children start to slowly transition into another great achievement of childhood – learning to consider the world mentally, by thinking about it. By six, children use basic logic and make simple inferences. They are able to tap into the stored impressions in their brains when they want to think about something. They become able to give plausible answers to *"What if?"* questions. These are the hallmarks of learning to use abstract thought.

One of the reasons public school starts at five or six is because they are waiting for children to think about the world in the abstract like older children and adults. The unspoken message is, *"When you perceive the world and think like we do, we can teach you."* Montessori and other good preschools, however, have shown for decades that with the right approach it is easy to help children facilitate their development of abstract thinking skills, along with building better brain nerve architecture, in the years from about 2 ½ - 6.

One way this is done is by providing experiences that include objects along with image-based materials like photographs and drawings, and by talking about things and reading to children until they are ready to read. Moving children back and forth along a path of: object – image – word – thought facilitates the development of abstract thought.

Circle

Experiences with round objects (top), lead to using image-based materials (middle), until finally a word (bottom) stimulates thoughts of curves and roundness.

Through experiences with objects, images, and written and spoken language, a child smoothly makes the transition to using abstract thought over a period of years.

Using educational apps

So, are tablet apps valuable? If so, when should we let a child use them? I believe high quality educational apps are valuable and appropriate learning materials for young children who are transitioning to abstract thought; providing that children have consistent access to hands-on learning materials and experiences in the earlier years and at the same time they are using apps. Both experiences are important.

How do we know when a child is making the transition to abstract thinking? The spontaneous development of an interest in letters, words, counting, and numbers is a great sign. When a young child starts to be able to relate to letters and numerals, as well as drawings of shapes, photographs, and other symbols and images, she is ready to start using high quality digital tablet apps. For these children, tablet apps become another way to deliver image – based learning experiences. They have the added bonus of being interactive, requiring critical thinking and memory, teaching real skills, and being a lot of fun. Tablet apps are the next step in the evolution of image – based learning materials.

Suggestions for tablet use:

- Limit tablet and all other screen time. Young children need to move their bodies and experience the world directly most of the time. Set clear limits and stick to them.

- Use parental controls. Monitor what your child is seeing.

- Work with your child on the tablet regularly. Play games, and let your child show you what he has learned. Have shared digital experiences.

- Use an iPad (like a used iPad2) and the best quality Apple educational apps. Android has a long way to go to match the quality of Apple's educational apps. The best educational apps are made for the iPad.

- Have your child use a stylus to prepare for writing.

Throughout this book you will find recommendations for high quality educational tablet apps. You can find over 200 recommended in the Montessori At Home! eBook (p.4). Common Sense Media is another good guide to apps.

Learning to read online

If you just don't have time, don't feel confident teaching, want to supplement your home activities with additional instruction, or if your child just loves online learning, there are a number of good sites for learning to read.

Starfall has numbered steps on their home page. **Reading Eggs** is a popular and reasonably priced online reading program, with an iPad app for tablet users. **Study Dog** is a popular site with a section just for parents. **Usborne** has a nice program. **Learn to Read Free** has good material which, as stated in their name, is free. **Reading Bear** is heavy into phonics, but they offer great online activities. **PBS Kids** is worth a look. The great homeschooling site **1+1+1=1** has many wonderful reading activities, many free or very inexpensive. Look under 'Kindergarten' and 'Learn to Read'. Using at least some online material is a great help in reinforcing your home reading activities.

When is my Child Ready to Read and Write?

Your child is ready to learn to write letters and numbers when she is working towards developing a writing grasp. All preschoolers are working towards this as they handle their toys and learning materials, even if we are not aware of it.

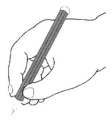

Tripod Writing Grasp

A writing grasp is developed over time by using a variety of hands-on materials that gradually develop small muscle control of the hand and fingers, including having constant access to drawing and tracing materials. Examples of these activities are shown here. Give them to your child regularly and let him practice with those he likes the best until his grasp has refined itself to close to the grasp pictured. More on this to come.

Your child is ready to learn to read when she starts showing spontaneous interest in letters and words, or in activities built around letters and words. When your child starts asking what words say when you read together, is showing an interest in letters, is becoming more aware of printed language, and is eager to do activities based around letters and words; that is the time to start the three step process shown here for helping your child learn to read.

If your child is 4 or 5 and has not shown too much spontaneous interest, start the three step reading sequence (p.56) and see how she responds. Not all children give clear outward signs, but most are ready for learning to read and write between ages 4-6.

Your child's naturally expressed interests are always your best guide to what materials and activities to provide. Children have an Inner Teacher guiding their growth and development in the early years. Throughout history, the Inner

Teacher has guided children to learn to walk, talk, use abstract thought, master basic life skills, develop independent personalities, and learn to function in this world, on a similar timeline, all over the planet.

By about age six, children develop into people suited to live in the time, place, and culture of their birth. They do this even without much help from adults, though providing some help is better. Learning to read and write is all part of this natural process, not an artificial educational task we impose on children's development.

Children are genetically programmed to learn to read and write. Acquiring these skills is a natural part of their development, Young children, at some point, start wanting to learn how to write and read. That is the time to help them.

Using worksheets

Many of us used worksheets all the time in school, so it is easy to assume that they are appropriate materials to use with young children. In moderation, perhaps; but it is very easy to overdo using worksheets.

Before age 5-6, children are in a period of life when healthy brain development requires hands-on and sensory experiences with the real world. This is why Montessori preschools, for instance, have low shelves filled with a huge variety of materials made using three dimensional objects.

Worksheets can be gradually used as a child develops the capacity for abstract thinking. Most children doing the pre-reading and pre-writing skills activities are 3-5 years old, so hands-on, object-based materials are what they need to use most of the time. It is also fine to work with images. Using the occasional worksheet if your child shows interest and enthusiasm is okay. Worksheets are perfect for writing practice for children learning to write letters.

Donna Young's site at **donnayoung.org**, under 'Handwriting', has all kinds of excellent worksheets to use when your child starts learning to write.

Okay, let's start with materials and activities to help your child develop pre-writing and pre-reading skills. Then we can move on to writing and reading.

Reading with Your Child Every Day

Shutterstock

Reading with your child every day is the single most important thing you can do to help your child become a successful reader.

Children imitate us. If you watch TV and hardly ever read, don't expect your child to be excited about reading. If you don't read much, start today. Let your child see you reading often. Talk with your spouse and others about what you read. Get excited about books. Read a novel, the newspaper, and magazines. Read on your tablet and computer. Go to the library together.

Reading should be practiced, valued, and encouraged in your family.

Read with your child every day from a variety of books your child finds interesting. Look for award winning books (p.87-89), do internet searches, and encourage your child to pick out books at the library, the bookstore, and the app store. As you two read together every day, you can point out interesting words, phrases, and sentences. If you have not laid this foundation, start reading daily with your child today. Point out words and talk about what they mean. When your child shows spontaneous interest in words, start the Reading Sequence (p.56). Family reading time creates an early interest in reading. There are things you can do to make reading time the best possible experience for your child:

Make reading time special

Make reading time a regular part of your daily routine. Let your child pick out books to read. Read with your child close or on your lap. Make reading time a warm, loving time of fun and discovery. Your child will associate reading with these positive feelings for years to come.

Animate the story, be dramatic

Shutterstock

Let out your inner child as you read. Make the story come alive by changing voices with the characters and acting out the emotions of the story. Be amazed when it takes an unexpected turn. Be animated and excited, and show this in how you read.

Encourage your child's participation

Ask your child what he thinks is going to happen next. Have him predict what the characters will do. Encourage your child to express ideas, questions, and observations.

Read books your child finds interesting

Your child will develop an interest in reading faster if she reads books she finds really interesting. Let your child pick out books at the bookstore. Check out the classic books listed starting on page 87. Let your child pick out what to read each day.

Read favorite books often & draw your child's attention to the print

Repetition encourages an interest in the print. This helps a child become comfortable with reading, build a sight word vocabulary, and imprint the text in her mind. By repeating favorite books, children gradually learn to start focusing attention on the print as well as the illustrations and the story line.

Talk about what you read

If it is a book your child has read before, see what she remembers about what happens in the story. If it is a new book, flip through it first and talk about what the book might be about. As you read, ask for your child's feedback on how the story makes him feel, what he thinks will happen next, his favorite and least favorite characters, whether animals really talk – anything you can think of. This will get your child thinking, and improve her comprehension.

Encourage your child to read

If your child wants to, let him take over reading a familiar book. If he veers off into his own version, let him go. His creative energies are being stimulated. If it is a familiar book, your child may soon be able to recognize some of the words.

Read from a variety of sources

Books, magazines, the iPad, signs, labels, tags – every bit of information registers in the early years. Let your child read the words he can and tell him what the rest say. Reading should evolve as a natural process, not on a deadline or with any stress. Use every opportunity to help your child learn to read.

Shutterstock

Reading with your child every day is the foundation for teaching your child to read independently. Here are more good ideas:

- When you read with your child, avoid following along under the words with a finger, unless it is to sweep your finger left to right to indicate the direction your eyes are taking as you read. Doing this once in a while helps your child get the left to right idea. Create left to right patterning whenever you can when doing the pre-reading and pre-writing activities (p.23).

- Read with a fluent, conversational style, as if you were speaking to someone. If your child wants to know what a word says or points to a word that is fine, talk about it and continue reading fluently. This models good reading habits for later. See p.75-76.

- Watch for signs that your child is getting tired or wants to do something different. When this happens, bring your reading to a positive conclusion and start again the next day or later that day.

- Be adaptable and flexible. If your child tires of one book, try another. Let your child pick books to read. Stop reading if your child really wants to do something else.

- Read Mother Goose and other children's rhymes and learn children's songs together. Poetry and songs have a natural rhythm that children love. Later, start pointing out the words.

- If your child asks a lot of questions or makes numerous comments about what you are reading, great! This means the story is simulating his brain. Take time to answer questions and discuss elements of the story and what it makes your child think of.

"Books are the quietest and most constant of friends; they are the most accessible and wisest of counselors, and the most patient of teachers."

Charles William Eliot

The Reading & Writing Sequences

Shutterstock

To give you a clear picture, here is a summary of how the writing and reading activities are sequenced:

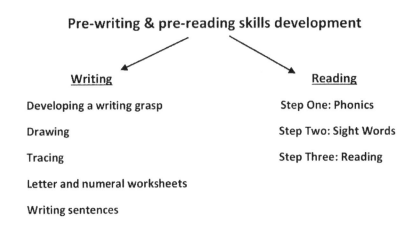

Pre-writing & pre-reading skills development

Writing	Reading
Developing a writing grasp	Step One: Phonics
Drawing	Step Two: Sight Words
Tracing	Step Three: Reading
Letter and numeral worksheets	
Writing sentences	

Children typically are ready to learn to write before they learn to read, so the sequences are listed separately. In reality, the activities will overlap. Many children start Step One of the Reading Sequence at roughly the same time they are learning to write letters. If this happens for your child, you can do both types of activities at the same time. Steps two and three of the reading sequence can start as the previous step is finishing up. Follow your child's interests and level of skills development and you will both be fine.

Pre-Writing & Pre-Reading Skills

Thumb up cutting at Shannon's Tot School

It is very important that young children have a chance to develop the skills required to write and read before they try to learn how. Having these skills in place is the difference between a smooth process and a struggle. My advice: do not ignore these activities and go right to writing and reading. These skills lay the foundation that makes writing and reading much easier to learn. Writing and reading require a few specific skills, including:

- Developing a writing grasp

- Visually differentiating between shapes and forms

- Learning left to right visual tracking

- Learning to reproduce line patterns

These skills can be developed with fun materials and activities, starting at around 2 1/2 – 3 years of age. If your child is 4 or older when you begin, present these activities and allow her to use them as much as necessary to be sure the skills are developed. These activities also lead nicely into learning about numbers, another common interest of young children.

Transfers

Transfer activities are used in all Montessori preschools. They are great for developing hand and finger control. Some can be extended to teach left-to-right visual tracking, counting, and other skills. Children love moving materials back and forth between containers. Allow plenty of practice with each material before moving on. Here is a sample sequence of transfer materials that will develop a writing grasp:

In the first material, water is moved back and forth between bowls with a small sponge, cut to fit the child's hand. This exercises the most primitive 'claw', or whole hand, grasp. Always include a towel and show your child how to clean spills using the sponge and towel. Demonstrate the transfer first for your child, including how to clean a spill. Sponging is also a science experience in capillary action. Comparing the weight of the sponge when dry and saturated exercises the baric (weight) sense.

When you set up an activity, let your child help. Handle everything slowly and carefully, like it is a Big Deal (which it is!). Demonstrate how to do the transfer first. Use slow, exaggerated hand movements, really take your time and put on a little show for your child.

"Do not tell them how to do it. Show them how to do it and do not say a word. If you tell them, they will watch your lips move. If you show them, they will want to do it themselves."

Maria Montessori

Rice poured back and forth between small, plain cups uses a 'C' shaped grasp and starts opposing the thumb to the other four fingers. Demonstrate how to pick up spilled grains and always encourage your child to pick up spills.

In the water transfer above, water with food coloring (your child's favorite color) is moved between bowls with a turkey baster. Squeezing the bulb can be done with a whole hand or opposed thumb grasp. Learning how to pick up and expel the water with control involves learning a new set of skills.

Pouring rice, and then water, between pitchers with handles and pouring lips creates new challenges. The thumb opposes the fingers and is used to brace against the handle for stability. The wrist is flexed and rotated to make the pour. This exercises the hand and finger muscles in new ways.

Next, plastic practice golf balls or whiffle balls (sporting goods section at a discount store) are moved between the depressions of an egg carton using kitchen tongs or small size plastic tongs. This directly opposes the thumb to the fingers, preparing the child for achieving a writing grasp. A good variation is to move large lego style blocks (Duplo) from a bowl to an egg carton with tongs. Handling a straight sided object is different than handling a sphere.

You can introduce counting and left-to-right visual tracking by setting the carton horizontally and writing the numbers 1-12 on both the balls and in the depressions of the carton, starting at the top left corner with 1. The bottom row starts with 7 in the left end depression. Your child finds the 1 ball, picks it up with the tongs, and places it in the 1 depression of the carton. Moving to the right, she repeats with 2, 3, 4, etc. Start over with 7 at the bottom left and continue to 12.

These activities do not have to be presented as self-contained materials, as is done in Montessori schools. Look for any opportunity to encourage your child to help in the kitchen with tools she can use safely. You can set up an impromptu activity at the counter or table and let your child pursue the activity while you are working in the area. This will help your child develop fine motor skills.

The next activity in this sequence uses tweezers to move small beads, beans, or crafts pom poms between small cups. This opposes the thumb to just two or three fingers, further refining the child's grasp. You can use multiple cups so your child can sort the objects by color or type (beans) as they are transferred.

Now, an eyedropper (medical section at discount store or pharmacy) is used to transfer water colored with food coloring between the same small cups. This requires adjusting the pressure of the thumb opposed to just two fingers.

Always provide a water resistant table mat, sponge, and a cloth so your child can clean up any spills. This is all part of the activity. Children do not see a difference between the parts of an activity. They are interested in doing everything they can.

Finally, peas or small beans are moved with the smallest measuring spoon of a set. This should be done using a proper writing grasp, as shown in the photo. Your child has now moved through a series of materials, with plenty of practice at each step, and gradually developed a writing grasp.

Using scissors

Learning to cut with scissors is a challenge. This child is starting out right, with safety scissors and a sheet of Playdoh. Playdoh is easier to cut than paper; and much more forgiving for a child using scissors for the first time. With enough practice, this child will move into free cutting card stock strips, sheets of paper, and finally along lines drawn on paper.

Photo: Montessori MOMents

Always encourage your child to use scissors '*thumb up – like shaking hands*'. Once a child has practiced with PlayDoh and is getting the hang of it, she can do these cutting activities, in order:

Free cutting with 1" wide strips of card stock

Free cutting with small (try 5" square) sheets of card stock

Cutting 1" wide card stock strips along parallel lines drawn across the strips

Cutting progressively harder line patterns and shapes

Top: Cutting strips of card stock along lines drawn across the strips. These strips have the numerals 1-5 on them to add math to the activity. Note the thumb is up, 'like shaking hands'.

Peaceful Parenting

Middle: A tray for cutting straws, along with a little box to hold the cuttings. Trays like this are perfect for displaying on low shelves in your child's room.

Counting Coconuts

Bottom: Cutting hearts. You can also print out the geometric shapes from your free printables (p.9) for cutting and learning the shapes.

The Activity Mom

There are line and shape cutting master sheets in your free printables (p.9). Print these out and make copies so your child will have them to practice cutting with. Your child can make a nice mobile by punching holes around the edges of the shapes and lacing a shoelace through them. Cutting out photos from magazines is also good work. Plenty of practice is required to master cutting complex shapes by turning and adjusting the paper in relation to the scissors. Your child may also move the scissors around the paper. Always provide child safe scissors until your child is older and shows consistent safety awareness.

Bead Threading

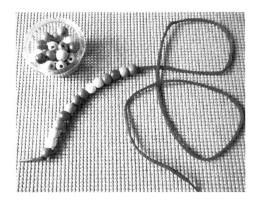

Bead threading is a fantastic activity. Put everything into an attractive little bowl or basket so your child can use the material any time. Watch younger children who put things in their mouths, as beads are easily swallowed. Best to wait until these children are older, or use jumbo beads that cannot be rolled down a toilet paper hole. Tie a knot on one end of the shoelace.

You can easily teach colors and basic counting with this activity. To train your child in left-to-right visual tracking, use two shoelaces, laid horizontally and parallel, one above the other. On the top string, you thread on beads in a color pattern, such as in the photo (blue, white, yellow, orange, red, violet, green). Your child now makes a matching pattern on the string below and names the colors going left to right.

Marbles & golf tees

You will need a block of floral foam (crafts store), a bag of golf tees, marbles, a couple of bowls, and a tray to hold everything. Let your child practice pushing in the tees straight so they will hold marbles. Next, help her as needed to make a straight line of tees and lay marbles on them. Count the tees left to right. With enough floral foam, your child can create shapes with the tees: square, triangle, rectangle, etc.

Photo: Pink and Green Mama blog

PlayDoh

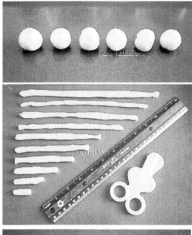

PlayDoh is a wonderful material for developing the fine motor skills needed for writing. Just pulling, rolling, squeezing, poking, and kneading playdoh is great muscle exercise. **Top**: Have your child roll similar balls and lay them in a line for counting from left to right. **Middle**: Help your child roll a few long snakes of playdoh. Provide a small ruler and show him how to measure off 1", 2", 3", etc. lengths and cut the snake into these lengths. Help as needed to show him how to make a graded set from shortest to longest. **Bottom**: Press out a sheet of playdoh and use a food container lid to cut out a square. Help your child measure and cut it into 2 and 4 identical pieces. This introduces counting and fractions.

Nuts and bolts

A collection of various sizes of nuts and bolts make a great fine motor material activity. Start with 3-4 bolts and nuts to fit, as in the top photo.

Next, get a set of bolts in decreasing sizes from ½" or ¾" diameter down, with washers and nuts to fit. As your child puts the washers and nuts on, he can grade the bolts from largest to smallest.

Other good fine motor materials include wooden blocks, Legos, and Unifix Cubes.

Sorting

Sorting objects according to their size, shape, color, and other characteristics is a great activity for building the visual recognition skills required for reading. Adding tools such as small cups, tweezers, tongs, and spoons to move the objects creates opportunities for fine motor skill development, as in the Transfers (p.24).

Wooden beads that differ only in their colors are sorted into smaller bowls using kitchen tongs to pick them up. Using 10 beads of each color leads naturally into counting opportunities.

Mixed beans (previous page, bottom) are sorted by variety, using a small measuring spoon to pick them up. This adds new fine motor challenges as the child learns to pick up just the beans she wants to.

Coins are sorted by type. This can easily lead into a math activity by learning the value of each coin (how many pennies in each) and exchanging the coins. Many materials can be used for sorting: metal washers of various sizes, different shapes of pasta, and paint color cards from the hardware store (get multiples of each of many different colors for sorting). When your child has experience sorting objects, try making an image sorting activity like this:

The Learning Ark

Images of living things and inanimate objects that belong on land, in water, or in the air are sorted under name cards with those categories. This takes the sorting experience another step into abstraction, preparing a child for reading. Other image sorting options include: Living / Non-living, Clothing (pants, gloves, hats, coats, shoes, etc), and Transportation (cars, planes, boats, bicycles, etc). Do internet searches and save the images you like for printing out on card stock. Make simple category name cards with a marker and index cards.

In your free printables (p.9) set, you will find nice Animal and Fruit sorting activities, using photos and with the name cards included.

Visual discrimination materials

Grading objects from largest to smallest, longest to shortest, and darkest to lightest is an excellent way to help 2-5 year olds build the visual discrimination skills that are essential for reading. The following are a few materials that work well at home.

Montessori Pink Tower

 The Pink Tower ($45 at Montessori Outlet online) is a classic material for 2-4 year olds. There are 10 cubes to stack and arrange horizontally and in other creative ways. The smallest cube (don't lose it!) is 1cm on all sides. Each successive cube gets 1cm larger up to the largest at 10cm on each side. One of the best ways to present this, and all grading materials, is to simply show your child how to handle the cubes carefully and let him explore. Spontaneous discoveries are usually the most powerful learning experiences.

If your child needs a little help, have her lay out the cubes on a small rug and ask, "*Can you find the largest cube?*" Have her set it to the side. Now ask, "*Can you find the largest cube of these that are left?*" When she finds this cube, have her center it over the largest cube and set it down on it. Continue this way until the Tower is built. The cubes can be arranged all kinds of ways. Show your child how to grade them horizontally, left to right to prepare for reading.

When your child has used the tower awhile, or with most 4-6 year olds, introduce the **Superimposed Figures** from Montessori Print Shop that are included with your free printables (p.9). Using graphic images and photos takes the experience another level into abstraction, preparing a child for reading. The cards can be stacked and arranged just like the cubes, with different effects, as in the second photo of an arrangement made using the printable squares, and the next photo shown using the circles included with the printables. Be sure to do some horizontal layouts made by going from left to right to reinforce this important visual tracking skill. The **Banana and Squirrel Grading** printables in your free set are more good materials for visual discrimination work.

Unifix Cubes

Unifix Cubes ($13 on Amazon) can be used for many wonderful learning activities with preschoolers, including making a set of rods to grade by size, as in the bottom photo. This leads naturally into counting the rods as they are built, adding one more each time, and bringing math into the activity. Try to make each new rod of cubes the same color for clarity at first. Using random colors can make identifying the longer and shorter rods more of a challenge; but makes counting easier.

Common household items, like a set of nesting measuring spoons and nesting bowls or food containers work well for size grading. With measuring spoons, get a set with as many spoons as possible, and similar in appearance except for their size. Get a set on a ring that allows you to remove the spoons for laying out at random, as in the photo. Socket sets can also be used for size grading:

Montessori Knobless Cylinders

The Montessori Knobless Cylinders ($68 at Montessori Outlet online) are wonderful for 2-5 year olds for exploring, building, and size grading. All kinds of arrangements are possible, most of which your child will discover just by playing with them. Grading the cylinder groups left to right from largest to smallest, shortest to tallest, and thinnest to thickest provides excellent visual practice for reading. You can sell the Pink Tower and Knobless Cylinders on Ebay when your child is finished with them and recover at least half their cost or more.

Another versatile, inexpensive size grading material can be made with straws (photo left). Cut five each in 1", 3", 5", 7", and 9" lengths and let your child organize them by size from a random group.

Cut straws only 1" difference in length, and then just ½", etc., to make this activity more challenging. Counting is easily introduced with this activity. Make sets of 10 of each size and have your child practice counting to ten as the straws are grouped and graded by size.

Color shades grading

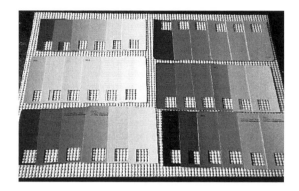

In your free printables set (p.9), you will find the **Color Grading Cards,** with 9 different colors and 6 shades of each color, from Montessori Print Shop. You can also make a set using paint sample cards from a paint or hardware store (photo). Find cards with 3-4 shades on a card, then look for the next card that picks up where that card leaves off, so you end up with 6-8 shades of each color. Get a mix of bright, primary and secondary colors (red, yellow, blue, green, brown, violet) and a few other nice colors in shades from darkest to lightest. Get colors where the shades vary distinctly; and others where the differences are more subtle. Store the cards rubber banded in color groups in a small food container, along with color name cards.

To show your child how to grade the cards, lay all the shades of one color out in a random group. Pick up the darkest and lightest shades. Show your child the shades and identify them as *darkest* and *lightest*. Lay those back down into the random group. Ask, *"Can you find the darkest one?"* Your child finds the darkest shade and sets it on the left side of the table or mat. Ask, *"Can you find the darkest one of those that are left?"* Your child sets this card just to the right of the darkest card. Continue until all the cards are graded, darkest to lightest going left to right.

Shapes & forms

Reading and writing both require a familiarity with basic shapes and forms. Experiencing these in their pure forms before trying to write is especially important and helpful. Recognizing shapes is a skill developed through progressive experience with solid shapes, flat shapes, and graphic images. These activities train a child's visual sense to recognize shapes and patterns, which translates into being able to recognize letters and numerals.

The **19 Geometric Solids from Learning Resources** (top) are nice wooden shapes for under $30. These help children absorb all kinds of information about geometric shapes just by handling them. The **Didax Easyshapes 3D Geometric Shapes** ($16) are an affordable set of solid shapes made of soft foam. There is a set of geometric solids shape names in your free printables set.

The **Montessori Mystery Bags with Geometric Shapes** (bottom), another great material for around $16, have pairs of most of the geometric solids, along with two great bags which can be used for many activities to develop a child's stereognostic sense: the ability to visualize an object by feeling it. Store materials like these on your child's shelves in nice basket, with a cloth to lay out for setting the shapes on.

A set of geometric shape names is included in your free printables (p.9). Activities with geometric shapes include learning and matching them to their names, sorting them by curved sided and straight sided, tracing their bases, and using the mystery bag to identify them by feel. You can also search the names on the internet and look for images of objects in the environment in those shapes.

Once your child has learned and handled three dimensional geometric shapes, introduce plane, or flat, shapes. Templates for making your own shapes, and a set of shape name cards, are included your free printables (p.9) set. Use these to make a nice set of shapes for your child's shelves.

Print these out onto colored paper but don't cut them out yet. Now, use paper spray glue to glue these sheets onto heavier cardboard or 14 pt. illustration board (arts & crafts store). Rough cut the shapes out first, then cut each exactly along the lines. Heavy scissors or shears work best. If you like, you can glue a small wooden knob (crafts store) onto each shape for a handle. Put your child's shapes in a little basket.

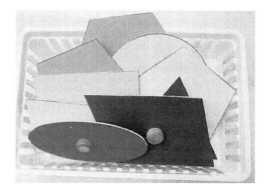

Your child can match the shapes with their names, say their names, feel the edges of each shape with her fingers, and trace the shapes onto paper to make an endless number of designs. Help him do an internet search for each shape to find common objects in each shape.

Many objects can be used for plane (flat) figure experiences. Large buttons, wooden shapes from a crafts store, and all kinds of objects around your home can be traced, like food container lids, glasses, and knick knacks. Your child can then match the objects to their tracings:

The Activity Mom

The **Melissa & Doug Shapes Puzzle** (Amazon) is a great introduction to geometric shapes for a 2-3 year old, offering fine motor work, language, and figure-ground matching experiences. **Pattern Blocks** are wonderful flat shapes that children can combine in all kinds of ways to make an infinite number of designs and all kinds of geometric shapes:

Chasing Cheerios

The **Melissa & Doug Pattern Blocks** are an excellent material. Your child can build free form shapes and match shapes to master tiles and design sheets. If your child loves these, you can get a set of 400 Pattern Blocks at Lakeshore Learning.

There is a wonderful online interactive pattern block activity at:

www.mathplayground.com/patternblocks.html

Download great free pattern block design mats here:

www.prekinders.com/pattern-blocks

Good iPad pattern block apps include **The Pattern Blocks** and **My First Tangrams**.

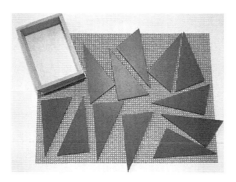

The **Montessori Blue Triangles** ($16) are a set of 12 blue, scalene, right angle triangles, stored in a nice wooden box. They can be combined to make all kinds of shapes and designs that give a child direct experience with geometry. Here are examples:

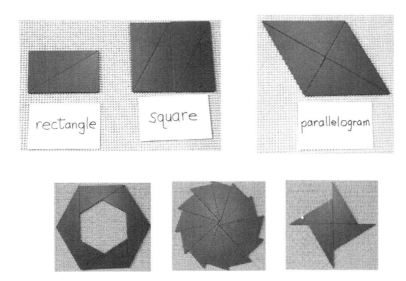

Safety Note: Montessori materials are made precisely, and often have sharper edges and points than typical children's toys. Always make sure your child uses them carefully. They should never be thrown, waved about, or handled roughly. Children in Montessori schools are supervised, and become accustomed to using all the materials with care. At home, it is often best to bring out materials like this as special projects when your child is calm and focused.

A set of **Blue Triangle Three Part Cards** from Montessori Print Shop is provided in your free printables set (p.9):

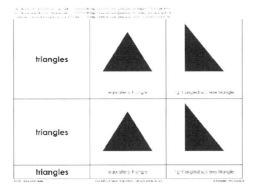

These are helpful in taking your child's shapes experiences another step into abstraction.

 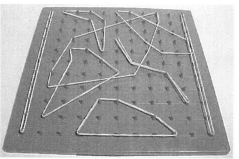

A **Geo Board** is a sheet of plastic with protrusions sticking out of it in a precise grid pattern for stretching rubber bands around. These can be made at home with cardboard or wood using pushpins or brads; but injury is possible when pushpins and brads work loose. I recommend an inexpensive plastic Geo Board from Educator's Outlet or Learning Resources.

Once your child has experimented and become familiar with stretching rubber bands over the nubs, see if she can duplicate the shapes from the geometric shapes set in your free printables (p.9). You can also provide colored rubber bands to highlight the sides of various shapes:

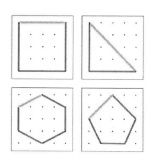 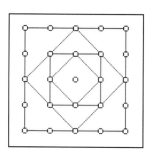

Geo Board is a nice, free iPad geo board app. **Mosaic HD** is another great shapes activities iPad app. At the sites below you will find fun interactive geo board tools:

www.mathplayground.com/geoboard.html

jmathpage.com/JIMSGeometrygeoboards.html

Printable shapes materials are the final step in your child's shapes work, and help take work with three dimensional shapes another step into the abstract. This directly prepares a child for recognizing printed letters and numerals. The next images show examples of materials available from **Montessori Print Shop**, a great source of all kinds of classroom quality preschool printables, the same ones used in Montessori schools.

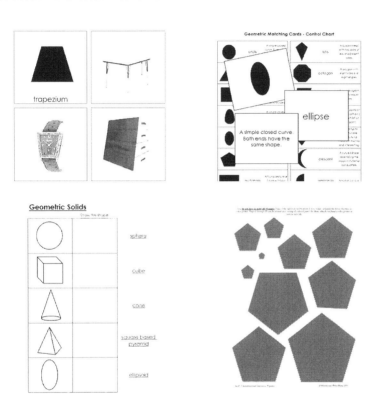

Top left: **Geometric Shape Sorting**. Top right: **Geometric Matching Cards**. Bottom left: **Geometric Shapes Worksheets**. Bottom Right: **Superimposed Geometric Figures.** The Superimposed Figures are included in your free printables set (p.9).

Good iPad apps for working with shapes include **Baby Games My First Shapes**, and **Shapes Toddler Preschool**.

Apps for building pre-reading skills

When a child is ready to use more abstract, image-based materials, mobile tablet and phone apps become excellent learning tools. There are a number of good Apple and Android apps that help children develop the visual skills required for reading and writing. Here are ideas:

Pick-up Sticks (iPad, Android) develops visual acuity and discrimination. The excellent **Touch and Learn - Emotions** (iPad) focuses attention on visual cues and develops visual discrimination while sparking conversations about emotions. **Labyrinth** (iPad, **Android**) requires visual concentration, eye tracking, planning, and fine motor skills. **Touch and Learn - ABC Alphabet and 123 Numbers** (iPad) reinforces letter and number recognition and listening skills. **Smart Fish Magic Matrix** is an outstanding sorting and visual app.

Bitsboard (iPad) deserves special recognition. This is an incredible app that, IMO, should be on every preschooler's iPad. It has all kinds of customizable picture, number, object, letter, and verbal recognition activities. One of the best apps for kids.

Kids Connect the Dots (Android) uses either numbers or letters to connect the dots (use lower case when using letters), and directs a child's visual attention to line drawings. **A Preschool Pattern Recognition Game** (iPad) helps establish left to right tracking while focusing attention on graphic forms. There is a kindergarten version, too. **Little Patterns Shapes** (iPad) is another patterning app that uses more abstract shapes. The great **Wood Puzzle Slider** (iPad) is a fun, engaging game with beautiful graphics. It requires visual focus, planning, and symbol recognition skills. **123 Domino** (iPad) is another beautiful game that requires increasing levels of color and pattern recognition.

Have your child use a **stylus** to help her develop a writing grasp. Tablet time should also be writing grasp development time.

"I've helped with more computers in more schools than anybody else in the world and I'm absolutely convinced that is by no means the most important thing. The most important thing is a person. A person who incites and feeds your curiosity; and machines cannot do that in the same way that people can."

Steve Jobs

Learning to Write

Shutterstock

Once your child is on the way to developing a writing grasp by using the materials and activities shown previously, including plenty of time spent free drawing, it is time to start working towards writing letters and numerals. Whenever your child also starts showing increased interest in letters and words, you can also start the three step Reading Sequence (p.56).

What if my child is having trouble developing a writing grasp?

First, be sure he has had plenty of opportunities to practice with the transfer and other fine motor materials. Make sure she has drawing materials available and uses them often. It is easy to underestimate how much practice it takes to develop fine motor skills. In Montessori schools, children are free to repeat activities as often as they like. Children often repeat specific materials very frequently for a period of time. This concentrated practice allows a child to master a skill and then move on. The Inner Teacher provides the motivation, and the environment needs to respond. There are simple devices that can be used for a short period of time to help children train their fingers to use a writing grasp:

Grip aids, like the one pictured from **Draw Your World**, help a child develop a writing grasp. Natural development is always best. These are only temporary aids for 5-6 year olds if they need them. Most children just need more time with materials that build hand and finger muscle control and coordination.

Tracing

Your child should regularly be drawing and using materials to develop a writing grasp. When she is able to control a pencil well enough, tracing becomes the next step in learning to write. It requires new kinds of hand and finger control, provides muscle memory for making curved and straight lines, and opens up another world of art possibilities. All kinds of objects can be used for tracing.

At the crafts store, pick up some wooden shapes. These are great for tracing. You can also trace these onto squares of illustration board and cut out the shapes with an Xacto knife or shears (heavy duty scissors), creating frames that your child can trace around the inside. This is a little easier at first than tracing around the outside of an object.

The **Primary Shapes Template Set** ($8, photo previous page) from Learning Resources is a wonderful tracing material that features classic geometric shapes.

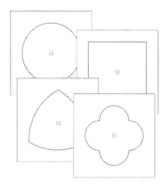

A beautiful set of traceable Montessori **Metal Inset Shapes Cards** (above) from Montessori Print Shop is included in your free printables set (p.9). Print these out onto colored paper and cut each one out as shown in the image. Use paper spray glue to glue these onto cardboard or illustration board and cut them out again. Carefully cut out each shape with a Xacto knife and glue a little wooden knob (crafts store) onto each. Now you will have a set of shapes that fit into identical shape frames and which can be traced around the outside of the shape or inside the shape frame, as with the $60 metal Montessori Insets.

Inexpensive plastic cookie cutters make great tracing shapes for tracing on the inside (easier) or the outside (harder). As with all tracing shapes, these can be superimposed to make all kinds of interesting designs.

Wooden crafts letters and numerals are perfect for tracing, and lead directly into writing. Try to find lower case as well as upper case letters. Lower case letters make up over 95% of everything we read, so children should work with them as much as possible.

Printable tracing materials

When your child has shown good ability to trace around both the inside and outside of objects, tracing worksheets are the next step in learning to write letters and numerals.

Donna Young's website (**donnayoung.org/penmanship/index.htm**) is a treasure. I highly recommend that you get familiar with the resources available there. Her fantastic free five week series of tracing worksheets take your child from tracing straight lines to tracing the lines used to make letters and numerals. Make as many copies as your child needs and introduce a new set of worksheets every week. Print out the cool Certificate of Completion to award your child when she finishes the 5 weeks of worksheets. A nice collection of **Preprinting Practice Sheets** from Montessori Print Shop is included in your free printables set.

You can download great free tracing practice sheets at:

www.lilbunnyhops.com/beginners_tracing_free_activities.html

Give your child plenty of practice with tracing worksheets and he will be ready to start writing letters and numerals.

Writing letters and numerals

It is likely that when your child is ready to learn to write letters and numerals, he will also be ready to start Step One of the Reading Sequence – Phonics. Since this involves learning one sound for each letter, it is very convenient to learn to write the letters at the same time. Many children start writing letters and learning the phonetic alphabet at about the same time, but they can be learned separately if that is how it works best for your child. Here are a few materials it will be handy to get together now:

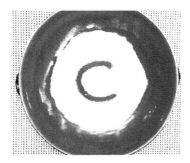

A wide, shallow pan with a layer of cornmeal is great for practicing writing. Just shake the pan lightly to 'erase' the letter and try again. Have the tray available when your child works with letter writing practice worksheets, so she can use both at the same time.

A set of Montessori Sandpaper Letters in lower case, print style ($30, previous page) is one of the most expensive items you will need to teach your child to read. These are still a bargain compared to many of the disposable plastic toys parents buy for children that teach absolutely nothing. Consider these an investment in your child's future. You can sell Montessori materials for half or more of their original price when your child is done with them, so these will only cost you around $15.

Decent alternatives to the Montessori letters include the **Didax Tactile Letters** ($15), and the **Ideal School Supply Lower Case Tactile Letters** ($9). These are sometimes unavailable, and are the smallest letters, but work for folks on a tight budget. The **Lower Case Tactile Letters from Lakeshore** ($15) are another good alternative to the Montessori sandpaper letters. **Desert Blossom Learning** has a nice set of lower case foam letters for $8 that you can mount on index cards. Get the blue consonants and red vowels set. You can substitute a block style letter a that you cut from foam yourself in the typestyle shown below.

If you use foam letters or printed letters, be sure the typestyle you use is as close to this as possible:

a b c d e f g h i j k l m n o p q r s t u v w x y z

This is Century Gothic, the basic, block style, lower case font. If you compare the letters above to those in the text of this book, you see a difference in the a and g letters, as well as little tips (serifs) and bulbs protruding from the other letters. This makes this font much more difficult to reproduce and complicates learning phonics. Stick with lower case, block style letters, as in the Montessori sandpaper letters and the other tactile letters recommended here.

Use lower case letters

Lower case letters make up over 95% of everything we read. I don't know where the habit began of teaching young children using capital letters, but stick primarily with lower case letters when learning to read. Once your child is into the Sight Words step, she can learn to write the capital letters.

Tactile letters are required for teaching the phonetic sound of each letter. As a child traces, looks at, and says the phonetic sound (p.61) of each letter, he gets tactile, visual, and auditory feedback. This helps get the information into long term memory. Tactile letters and numerals are also great muscle memory practice materials for a child learning to write.

Tracing tactile letters

Infomontessori.com

The first activity is to have your child trace the tactile letters with the first two fingers of his dominant hand while saying the name of each letter. He should then make the letters in the cornmeal tray with a finger. If you are doing Step One of the Reading Sequence (p.60) at the same time, you can have him say the phonetic sound of each letter also. Read more on that at the Step One section (p.60).

It is a good idea to coordinate your child's letter tracing with the sequence of phonetic sounds shown in the Step One section; and also with the letter writing practice worksheets you are using.

Letter writing practice worksheets

When your child gets to this point, learning to write letters and numerals is a matter of regular practice with worksheets and tablet apps. Writing requires being able to accurately and consistently reproduce a set of line drawings – the symbols we call letters and numerals.

Make practice time a routine part of your child's day, perhaps with a reward at the end if necessary, like a favorite healthy food or some extra tablet app time.

Notebooks like the **Mead Lower Case Letters Dry Erase Book** are used with dry-erase markers for repeated practice writing letters, and save on paper. The one shown was $3 at WalMart, look around for the best price.

The excellent **100 Sight Word Mini-Books** from Scholastic provides writing practice while teaching many common sight words. Your child can also make cute little books to read, nice!

DonnaYoung.org has a page about the beginning handwriting letters at:

donnayoung.org/penmanship/beginning-manuscript.htm

There are manuscript handwriting lessons with arrows, and a handy set of manuscript animations that show how to write each letter. Also offered are wonderful worksheets for learning cursive writing. Cursive writing is actually a bit easier to learn at first, so let your child give it a try.

Handwritingworksheets.com is another super resource. You can make your own custom worksheets with whatever letters or words your child wants, including their name, favorite foods, pet's name, etc.

Kidslearningstation.com has many nice worksheets, including sheets for each letter and numeral.

At **www.readtoday.net**, choose your language and you can print out free letter writing guides.

For children learning their sight words (p.76), writing words is one of the best ways to learn them. Use sight words for writing practice whenever possible.

Writing practice with tablet apps

Intro to Letters

Learning to use abstract thought is a critical developmental process that picks up steam from 3-6. Younger children require solid objects and other sensory input most of the time, so screen time should be minimal. As a child gets to 5-6, she becomes more able to use the sensory impressions collected earlier in her brain to start using abstract thought, like older children and adults.

Once a child has progressed far enough into developing abstract thought to be interested in learning to read, tablet apps become great options for learning. A tablet can be used for practicing writing, as long as your child uses a writing stylus. A stylus encourages the development of a writing grasp. Many children like the **Mini Alloy Stylus** (**www.stylusshop.com/products/mini-alloy-stylus**):

This stylus is sized and weighted for children and has a grip that encourages a proper writing grasp. You can also find cheaper ones that work almost as well. Consider a stylus essential equipment for a child writing on a tablet. Learning to write requires an instrument.

There are many good iPad apps for writing practice. **Montessori Letter Sounds** has script and cursive options, and introduces the phonetic alphabet and initial word sounds. Writing can be done on lined 'paper', tracing over guides, and freehand in a sand tray. **Write On** lets your child practice capital and lower case letters and writing words, and has a blank, lined board for practice. **Approach to Montessori: Numbers** allows practice with writing numerals and serves as an early math app. **LetterForms** is a nice, simple app that allows children to practice writing capital and lower case print and cursive letters. The too cool for **Letter School** app entertains while teaching your child to write.

Good Android tablet apps include **Writing Numbers,** which provides practice writing numerals and counting. The excellent **Kids Handwriting Grade K** lets a child write sight words, which is a great way to learn them. **Phonics and Handwriting** allows your child to write phonetic words and practice handwriting. Focus on lower case letters. **Magic Slate HD for Tablets** gives your child a place to freely draw and write letters and numbers. You can also use it later for math problems and other teaching activities.

Whether using worksheets or tablet apps, or, ideally both, learning to write letters is a matter of regular practice. Make a big deal when your child writes letters nicely. Hang her worksheets on the fridge. Let her copy her name and hang that up. Find all the ways you can to celebrate your child's writing achievements. We all love positive feedback!

One thing almost all children love to learn is how to read and write their own name. Make an ongoing project of this as your child uses apps and does reading activities. Making your own books (p.93) is a great way to encourage writing. Have your child dictate the contents of the book, one sentence at a time, and write this down in lower case, block style print, like the Century Gothic font (p.51). Now, have your child practice writing the sentences, using your writing as a guide. You can make a full sheet of text in dotted lines for your child to trace over to practice writing at:

www.worksheetworks.com/english/writing/handwriting.html

This is a nice way to help your child write entire paragraphs, which is wonderful preparation for reading the words right afterward.

The Three Step Reading Sequence

Phonics

Sight Words

Reading

Let's learn to read! The three step process shown here gives you a clear sequence of activities and materials for helping your child learn to read. Getting through all three steps can take anywhere from a few months to a couple of years, every child is different. How long it takes is not what is important. Your goals should be to give your child a positive, successful introduction to reading, to help him learn to start reading independently, and to make your child a lifelong reader. Here is a summary of the three steps of the Reading Sequence:

Step One: Phonics

At first, written language to a child is a series of meaningless symbols. The Phonics step gives your child a 'hook' into language by learning something reasonable: one sound for each letter. These sounds are then used to build words and simple sentences. Your child discovers he can do this stuff!

Step Two: Sight Words

Your child now learns to recognize common words as soon as she sees them – on sight. This is how we all read. In the Phonics step your child combined letters to make words. In this step, your child combines words to make sentences and read them.

Step Three: Reading

Nothing builds reading skill like reading. Building on the foundation of the first two steps, your child continues learning more sight words while reading simple books. As his skill increases, so does the level of challenge of the books he reads. From here on out your child simply reads, reads, reads.

This simple three step sequence uses the best of multiple approaches to teaching reading, in a logical sequence that fits with how children learn written language. It has been used successfully to teach many children to read, and you can use it with your child, too.

How long will it take to get through the three steps?

This depends on factors such as your child's readiness and interest, the amount of time your child spends on the activities, how often you have been reading to your child, and whether you follow the activities as shown. Most children, given adequate time to practice with the activities in an environment where reading is practiced, valued, and encouraged, are reading basic books in 3-9 months. Some will start reading sooner, others may take a couple of years.

Take your time, especially during the Phonics and Sight Word steps. These set the stage for reading. Rushing through them will leave your child high and dry – and frustrated – when he tries to read even simple books later. Make sure your child really understands phonics and knows at least 100 basic sight words before moving into early reader books. Do as many of the activities shown here as you can on a regular basis. Your child will still need help regularly when stumped by a word as he starts reading his first books. Sometimes we can forget what a challenge it is to learn to read!

The time it takes for your child to be reading well is not the most important thing. Your goal should first be to give your child a successful, positive introduction to written language. You are laying the foundation for a lifetime of reading, so it is important to keep things positive and create opportunities for success with activities your child enjoys.

Many children spend the bulk of their time developing pre-reading and pre-writing skills, and then progress pretty quickly through the actual writing and reading activities once they start. If your child does not show any special interest in reading herself until age 5, start the specific writing and reading activities then. You can work on the earlier skills development activities in the meantime.

Should we do activities on a schedule?

You have to decide what works best for your child. It is important to keep things positive and fun. You definitely want to avoid making your child feel like she is doing drudge work! Be patient, be positive, and encourage your child's efforts.

The best approach is to have materials displayed on low shelves in your child's room for easy access whenever your child is interested. Spontaneous interest is always the best starting point for preschoolers. If a child has a variety of materials always available, she will be more likely to find something of interest on any given day.

Chasing Cheerios

Ideally, your child will show interest and self-motivation for reading activities. Keeping the materials and activities your child is currently working with easily available and in view will increase their use. It is fine to suggest working with reading activities, especially once your child starts the phonics step. Once your child starts the writing and reading activities, as long as you do it positively, there is nothing wrong with setting a goal of working with the activities for a reasonable period of time every day.

What if my child does not want to do these activities?

It is always best to follow a preschooler's naturally expressed interests. Most children enter a sensitive period for developing their written language skills between ages 3-6, and especially from 4-6. Not all children, however, outwardly express this by demonstrating an interest in letters and words.

The first step is always to be sure your child has used the pre-reading and pre-writing activities to develop the necessary skills to be able to write and read. Provide these materials as shown and let your child progress to close to a writing grasp and into visual discrimination activities with solid and image – based materials. Children instinctively know if they can handle a material or activity. If they have the skillset, they will be confident. If not, they will shy away or get frustrated, both of which can shut down your reading and writing activities.

With a four year old who has not shown any particular interest in letters and words yet, try tracing the tactile letters with her and see if she shows an interest in this. If so, you can start the Phonics step. If not, put it away and do other activities, such as the pre-reading and pre-writing activities. Nothing is ever gained by pressuring a young child into specific activities. My best advice: be patient, be positive, and encourage your child's efforts. Also, avoid comparing your child to other children. Learning is not a competition or a race.

Once the skills are in place and the interest is there, children often progress through the reading and writing activities pretty quickly. Inner motivation and interest are the key. Your child may not show spontaneous interest in reading until age 5. That is fine, just start the Reading Sequence activities then.

Many children do reading activities regularly from age 4 on, but seemingly without intense enthusiasm, just kind of plodding along. Then, in the space of a few weeks, they start reading everything in sight. Montessori called this the 'explosion into reading'. The pattern is quite common in many areas of child growth and development. Periods of seemingly slow growth are punctuated by a short burst of intense development.

During the quieter periods, parents may wonder if their early learning activities are having a positive effect. Rest assured, everything we do with our kids has a big impact – both positive and negative. Young children are in a uniquely formative period of human life. Their brain nerve architecture and personalities are being formed from their experiences every day.

If your child needs some positive prompting, check out the ideas for encouraging reading on p.94-96. Above all else, keep your activities positive and fun. Leaning in the early years should always be a joyous series of explorations, discoveries, and successful achievements in learning new skills.

Okay, let's get on to the first step in our three step reading sequence: Phonics.

Step One: Phonics

The goals of this step are to give your child successful first experiences with written language by:

- **Learning one sound for each letter**

- **Building words using those sounds**

- **Learning simple blended sounds**

- **Reading books that use mostly phonetic words**

Early success with phonics sets the tone for continued success with written language. So, why not continue on with it like many reading programs do? Using phonics as the main approach for learning to read can cause a few problems. The English language is largely non-phonetic. Trying to figure out every word phonetically can drive a child crazy! Another problem is that an overemphasis on phonics can lead to a choppy, word-by-word approach when a child tries to sound out every word. This can lead to a non-fluent reading style.

In this reading sequence, we use phonics to give a child a successful introduction to written language, and initial success in building words and reading simple sentences and phonetic readers. This gives a child a feeling of success, and enthusiasm for continuing on with reading. Phonics has then served its purpose and we move on to sight words. We'll talk more about this as we go on.

Learning the Phonetic Alphabet

Your child's first goal is to learn one sound for each letter. The sounds are the short vowel sounds and the basic consonant sounds. Together, they are called the Phonetic Alphabet. Here they are:

a	As in apple	n	As in nut
b	As in bat	o	As in off (sounds like 'aw')
c	As in cat	p	As in pet
d	As in dog	q	As in quit (sounds like 'qw')
e	As in elephant	r	As in red
f	As in fog	s	As in sit
g	As in gum	t	As in top
h	As in hat	u	As in up (sounds like 'uh')
i	As in if	v	As in victory
j	As in jet	w	As in wet
k	As in Kentucky	x	As in box (sounds like 'ks')
l	As in lap	y	As in yellow
m	As in mat	z	As in zoo

Search the web and you will find endless ways of teaching these sounds. Before you buy a ton of materials, remember: Montessori preschools use just a few materials for this and their children learn to read well and quickly. The important thing is to help your child master each step and move on. Used positively and consistently, the materials and activities here will do the job.

It is fine to teach your child the names of the letters, but it is the *sound* of each letter that we are concentrating on. Materials you will need for this step include:

Tactile Letters (p.50-51)

Initial sounds printables (p.64-65)

Movable alphabet letters (p.68)

Phonetic Readers (p.72-74)

I suggest gathering these materials first so you are ready.

Of the many ways to teach children the phonetic alphabet, the **Montessori Three Step Lesson** is one of the very best. This technique, combined with practice writing letters and using printable materials to reinforce the sounds is, IMO, the best way to teach children the phonetic alphabet.

The Three Step Lesson (not to be confused with the three step reading sequence) is a technique Maria Montessori developed to help children get information into their long term memory. It may seem complex at first, but once you see the steps and practice it, you will see that it is really pretty simple. The Three Step Lesson is used in all Montessori schools, is easily learned by parents and teachers, and can be used to teach children the name of just about anything.

Doing a Three Step Lesson

Here is how to do a Three Step Lesson to teach the phonetic sounds of the letters m, a, and t:

Step One: Identification

In this step we show the child each letter, one at a time by itself, and tell the child what sound each letter makes. We use **tactile letters** (p.50-51) for this. The child traces the letter with the first two fingers, while looking at it and saying its sound. This provides visual, auditory, and tactile impressions.

 "This says 't'." Trace the letter, look at it, and say the t sound (as in top). Now your child does the same. Put the t away and get out the a. Remember: t just says 't', not 'tuh'.

 "This says 'a'." Trace, look at the letter, and say the a sound (as in apple). Hand it to your child and have him do the same. Put the a away and get out the m.

 "This says 'm'." Trace, look at the letter, and say the m sound (as in milk). Hand the letter to your child and let her do the same.

Provide a cornmeal tray (p.50) and let your child practice 'writing' each letter in the cornmeal as you do their sounds.

Step Two: Recognition

Now you present all three letters to your child and ask her to identify them:

 *"Can you show me the m?"* Child points to it. *"Where is the a?"* Child points to it. *"Which letter makes the t sound?"* Child points to it. Now, have your child close his eyes as you rearrange the letters and repeat the process.

 *"Can you show me the a?"* Child points to it. *"Where is the t?"* Child points to it. *"Which letter makes the m sound?"* Child points to it.

Repeat this at least two more times. Play games, like putting the letters on a table across the room and asking your child to get each letter in turn. Be sure to switch roles and let your child ask you to point out the letters by their sounds. Playing these games in Step Two is when the information makes its way into your child's long term memory.

Step Three: Recall

 "What sound is this?" Child says sound.

 "What sound is this?" Child says sound.

 "What sound is this?" Child says sound.

If your child does not remember the letters in steps two, or their sounds in step three, just go back to step one and start over. If your child gets frustrated at any point, immediately bring the activity to a positive conclusion and try again another day. The important thing is to help your child have success with learning the sounds. If you find that three letters at a time is a bit much, try using two.

Note: in steps one and three the letters are presented by themselves, one at a time. Only in step two do we present all the letters together.

Do Three Step Lessons with all the sounds, 2-3 letters at a time, in the order below. Remember: consonants just say their <u>single sound</u>, not 'buh', or 'guh'.

u b c s o h g r e n p i f
j l d v w y z x k q

Reinforcing the phonetic sounds

There are many ways to reinforce these sounds and help your child learn them.

The lovely **Phonics Sounds and Picture Sorting** material from Montessori Print Shop has control charts, work charts, 72 picture cards, word lists, and complete instructions. The pictures show objects whose names start with the phonetic sounds. As your child learns each group of sounds, get out those letters and their associated pictures and let your child sort and categorize the images based on the first sound in their names.

The **Initial Sound Choice Cards** from Montessori Print Shop are included in your free printables (p.9) set:

More initial sounds materials are available at these sites:

resources.sparkleplus.co.uk/sb370.pdf

www.galacticphonics.com/cvc/resources/cvcpics.pdf

thehelpfulgarden.blogspot.com/2011/10/beginning-letter-sound-word-walls.html

There are a number of good tablet apps for reinforcing and learning the phonetic letter sounds. **Starfall ABC's** (iPad, iPhone) is a simple, great app. **Phonics Consonants Free** (iPad) has great activities that also teach sight words. **ABC Pocket Phonics** (iPad) offers phonics and letter writing practice, along with early word building. **Kids ABC Phonics** (Android) lets children learn and manipulate letter sounds, as well as make words (I told them about the capital letters in the word building activity, we'll see if they change it). **ABC Read Write Phonics** (Android) is a pretty good app that also provides writing practice. **Little Reader Three Letter Words** (iPad) is a great introduction to beginning word sounds using actual words.

I highly recommend using all these various resources to reinforce letter sounds in different ways. Teaching by using a variety of experiences about the same topic is called 'immersion'. This is much more effective for most children than using only one method.

Phonetic Word Building

The next step in Phonics is to make words using the sounds your child has learned. It is really fun when you see a child get excited about being able to sound out and make real words, and then read them. This is when a child sees that he is really learning to read.

The words your child builds at first are called **CVC** words, for consonant – vowel – consonant. Examples: cat, mat, bun, ten, etc. You can start word building with your tactile letters (p. 50-51). Soon you will want a set of a few each of individual letters on little cards. You will find printable letters for this in your free printables (p.9).

When your child has learned m, a, and t, and the first six letters on page 64 (through h), it is time to have her build her first words. This is a big moment! Get a picture of a cat and the sandpaper letters **c**, **a**, and **t**.

Review the word with your child, saying it slowly so your child hears each individual sound: "**C - a - t, cat**." Have your child say the word and sound it out.

Lay out the letters in a random way and ask, emphasizing the **c** sound, "*What sound do our mouths make first when we say* **c** - at?" Let your child respond that it is the **c** sound. Have him set the **c** to the left side of your work area.

"*What sound do our mouths say next when we say* c - **a** - t?" Emphasize the short a sound. Your child finds the **a** and sets it to the right of the **c**.

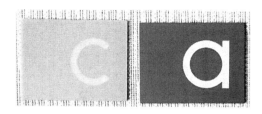

"What is the last sound our mouths say when we say c - a - <u>t</u>?" Let your child find it and set the **t** at the end of the word.

Point to the sounds and say each sound, not the letter names: "**C - a - t, cat**." Run your finger quickly left to right along the letters and say "**Cat**." Have your child do the same.

Make a big deal out of this - your child just built a word! As your child learns more phonetic sounds, he can build the words below.

cat	can	cub	bug	bun	bat
sun	mug	rug	tub	hat	map
hen	nut	pot	net	pan	cab
mop	hog	pen	ten	cap	pug

It helps to find pictures of these things on the internet so your child has a visual image to relate to when building these words. You can also look for little plastic and rubber figures of a dog, cat, pig, can, pot, pan, etc., at a crafts store to use as word building prompts. Give your child lots of practice with this important skill. Be very positive and patient, and encourage his efforts.

A set of magnetic lower case letters for the refrigerator make word building activities easy to do anytime you and your child are in the kitchen.

Now it is time to print and cut out a few Moveable Alphabets so your child has more letters to work with. This moves your child away from the large sandpaper letters to smaller ones in preparation for reading. There is a master sheet printable for making moveable alphabets in your collection of free printables (p.9). Montessori Print Shop offers beautiful Montessori Movable Alphabet Letters. Keep your child's letters in little boxes or envelopes labeled with the letters in lower case print.

Make lots of CVC words as your child learns the remaining sounds of the phonetic alphabet. Do different kinds of activities along with word building, like writing, matching, and spelling the words. Here are a few good resources:

CVC word lists: **www.keepkidsreading.net/docs/cvcwordlist.pdf**

Free CVC word lists: **whysospecial.com/tag/free-cvc-word-list/**

Wonderful Free CVC printables are available at these sites:

www.3dinosaurs.com/printables/learningtoread/wordfamily.php

www.eslprintables.com/vocabulary_worksheets/phonics/cvc_words/

www.galacticphonics.com/cvc/cvcwords.htm

Say each word and let your child find the letters to make it without looking at the word. After your child has built CVC words for a while, use the printed words for sight word practice. Show them to your child as flash cards. This prepares your child for the Sight Words step.

The **Little Stars - Word Wizard** iPad app is fun and provides practice with identifying simple words and beginning and ending sounds. When your child is getting good at making CVC words, you can introduce larger phonetic words. Notice that each letter in these words says its phonetic alphabet sound. Your child will probably need some help with these to carefully sound them out and build each word using the moveable alphabets.

Building larger phonetic words

When your child is getting good at making CVC words, you can introduce larger phonetic words. Notice that each letter in these words says its phonetic alphabet sound. Your child will probably need some help with these at first to sound them out and build the words using the moveable alphabets. Here are some words to build:

must	grab	trot	flop	slip	band	west
dust	blast	crop	soft	stamp	split	crisp
hasp	past	frog	cost	sand	drink	best
plan	last	camp	plastic	swim	frantic	trip
drag	snap	stand	blend	pond	glob	lips
cramp	trap	hand	lamp	flag	bank	stab
stub	mend	bend	send	tent	swept	crept
slept	link	milk	drip	gift	mist	wink
twist	frost	pond	drop	stop	cost	strip
melt	spend	bunk	skunk	trunk	drum	plum

Find more large phonetic words at these sites:

traintoread.com/Phonetic_Word_List.pdf

www.montessorimom.com/phonetic-word-list/

Reading Bear is a wonderful free, nonprofit site. Register for free and you have access to their entire catalogue of excellent phonics and word building resources. Be sure to donate to these great folks, if you can.

Tablet apps for word building

There are many great apps for word building, and for learning to read in general. I highly recommend tablet apps at this point in a child's reading development. These are some of the simplest yet most effective tools parents and teachers have for teaching reading skills in a personalized, fun way that allows each child to achieve success in their own way at their own rate. Here are some to consider:

Montessori Crosswords (iPad, Android) app. This great app provides practice making three letter and larger phonetic and non-phonetic words & consonant blends, has an option to focus on a single sound, and a moveable alphabet for free word building.

ABC Spelling Magic Short Vowel Sounds and **ABC Spelling Magic 2** (iPad) have options for building CVC words using the short vowel sounds as well as double consonant sounds.

Bitsboard (iPad) has CVC boards for each short vowel sound. Each board has flash card, photo touch, and word building options.

ABC Pocket Phonics (iPad) provides letter writing and word building practice as it guides your child through writing and making words.

Phonics Make a Word (iPad) allows building 3 letter CVC words.

Using these resources and your moveable alphabets, practice word building with your child until she knows most of the phonetic alphabet and is getting good at sounding out and building the larger phonetic words.

Next we work on common blended sounds before moving on to sight words.

Blended Sounds

Sequencing Note: You can start reading phonetic readers (p.72-74) while your child is learning the blended sounds. This keeps things moving along. Your child will be done with phonics after this last piece.

The last step in our Phonics work is to help your child learn to recognize common blended sounds, also called diagraphs. I don't get heavily into phonics, so I just call them all blended sounds, meaning two or more letters making a new sound together. If you search online for resources on blended sounds and diagraphs you will find a bewildering sea of phonics worksheets, videos, software, phonics programs, etc. I list some useful resources here.

Why we stop with phonics after this

Phonics devotees try to break down almost every word into single and blended letter sounds, and then put them back together. To promote this approach, they isolate out all kinds of letter combinations that are not really blended sounds at all. For example, bl in the word blue still says the two separate sounds, b, and l, not a new blended sound. The only true blended sound in the word is ue (oo). The letters dr in the word drip say d, then r, not a new blended sound. This is an example of how phonics starts to become an ineffective approach.

Encouraging a child to always sound out words also results in a choppy, word-by-word approach to reading as the child tries to decipher each individual word before continuing. This disrupts a child's ability to read fluently. Also, many English words are simply non-phonetic (it's a weird language). For these reasons, I only use phonics for one more step to teach your child the basic blended sounds. After this, phonics has served its purpose and we move on to sight words.

Here are examples of basic blended sounds to cover with your child:

th ch ck ph sh ing ion oo ee ie ow oy aw ea

Here are some excellent online resources for printables and games for teaching your child the basic vowel and consonant blended sounds:

bogglesworldesl.com/vowel_combinations.htm

bogglesworldesl.com/consonantdigraphs.htm

www.tlsbooks.com/englishworksheets3.htm

www.enchantedlearning.com/consonantblends/

Reading Bear (**www.readingbear.org/**) is a totally free, nonprofit site with all the blended sounds phonics materials you could ever want. Highly recommended.

ABC Phonics Word Family Writing HD is a super iPad app for learning blended sounds, writing practice, and sight words.

Also, if you want to teach your child about silent e, that's fine. The rule is that if a word has a silent e on the end, the vowel in that word says its own name, as in cake, cute, tone, bake, snake, etc.

Phonetic Readers

Starfall's Learn to Read readers

Your child has learned the phonetic alphabet, built phonetic words, and is learning basic blended sounds. Now it is time to put these new skills to work and read something! This step gives your child the great thrill of actually reading books. It is the absolute best platform for sending your child into reading with a positive, successful attitude, which is the goal of the Phonics step.

Sequencing Note: When your child has successfully read a few phonetic readers, you can start on the easiest sight words in the next step. This keeps things smoothly humming along as one step blends into the next.

To make it easy and give your child success, we read simple books that contain mostly phonetic words. That way, your child can sound out words she does not recognize. There are many apps, online resources, and paperback phonetic reader books. Here are some of the best for you to choose from:

Starfall (www.starfall.com) is a wonderful site. They have 4 steps listed right on their home page that any child can follow to learn to read. The **Starfall Short Vowel Pals** boxed set of phonetic readers makes a perfect choice for your child's first books to read on her own. These have been the first reading books of countless children, and your child will succeed with them, too. The **Starfall Learn-To-Read** books (photo previous page) are a great boxed set of first reading books. For tablet users, the **Starfall Learn to Read** iPad app has all their Learn to Read first readers in eBook format.

Miss Rhonda's Readers (www.missrhondasreaders.com) are excellent first reading books. They are organized into sets and offer supporting materials like word cards. These are many parent's top choice for first readers.

The **Bob Books** (Amazon) are classic first books that have launched many children into reading. There are 5 sets in the series, and other Bob Books available, also, all from Scholastic, one of the best suppliers of reading materials. The **Bob Books apps** bring the Bob Books to your iPad. There is an extensive collection of Bob Books printables available free at:

www.3dinosaurs.com/printables/learningtoread/bobbooks.php#set1

Rhyme To Read

Two educators, Lynn Klaiman and Sara Hines, created a very nice iPad phonetic reader app called **Rhyme To Read**. The app has a friendly interface, and includes 20 individual phonetic eBooks with titles like Ben, Chip, The Sock, and Tuck and Buck. The whole series covers all the common consonant and short vowel combinations, with the emphasized and repeated sounds in each book shown in color. There are simple instructions, and the books have a clean graphic look, with pleasing, simple illustrations that tell a story but do not distract from a focus on the words. This is a nice digital app option.

Download free printable phonetic readers at: **www.freephoneticreaders.com**

Encouraging fluency

As soon as your child starts reading phonetic readers, it is time to stress fluency. Encourage your child to read as if she were speaking to someone. Encourage him to avoid following under the words with a finger and reading one-word-at-a-time. This may be necessary at first and to sound some words out, but these tactics lead to a choppy reading style. Model fluent, smooth reading for your child and encourage her to read that way.

If your child stops to sound out a word, that's fine. Have her then read the entire sentence fluently, as if she were speaking to someone. If your child reaches a word he cannot figure out, simply tell him what it says so that his reading is not interrupted for too long. Use this technique whenever you read together. If your child stumbles on a word, just tell her what it says so she can keep reading. A smooth, fluent reading style takes practice from the start. Here are more ideas for encouraging fluency in your child's reading:

Do paired reading. You read a sentence fluently and then your child reads the same sentence the same way.

Re-read for fluency. If your child needs help on a word or stops to sound a word out, that is fine. Once all the words in a sentence are deciphered, have your child re-read the sentence fluently, as if speaking to someone. Read sentences and paragraphs over again, seeking a fluent reading style.

Encourage silent reading. Have your child read a story or paragraph silently, and then tell you what she read. Ask her questions about the text and story.

Read poetry. Poetry has a naturally fluent style. Read books with your child like The Random House Book of Poetry for Children, and The 20th Century Children's Poetry Treasury.

Use a recorder. A digital recorder or a tablet recording app is a perfect way to help your child learn to read fluently. Record each of you reading, and practice increasing your child's fluency.

Get audio books. Audio books are wonderful for modeling fluency. Your child can follow and read along with the audio track. Listening allows your child to absorb how excellent readers read and incorporate their fluency into his own reading.

"The fluent reader sounds good, is easy to listen to, and reads with enough expression to help the listener understand and enjoy the material."

Charles Clark

Step Two: Sight Words

Phonics gave your child a successful start with reading, but it is time to move on. Now we help your child learn to recognize words when she sees them, because that is how we read. In phonics, your child learned letter sounds and then used them to build words. In the Sight Word step, your child learns to recognize words, and then uses them to build sentences.

So, which words should you help your child learn? Luckily, there are established lists of the majority of the words found in all children's books and early reading books. These lists are the place to start. They are called the **Dolch Words** and the **Fry Words**. Search them online for all kinds of ideas.

Paul's House

Using these lists, play games and do different activities to help your child recognize and say these words when she sees them. This leads naturally into reading the words in sentences and books. Here are the Dolch Words, categorized into numbered groups to help you sequence through them:

Group 1	Group 2	Group 3	Group 4	Group 5	Group 6
the	at	do	big	from	away
I	look	what	now	want	saw
was	out	get	very	put	ran
for	we	my	ride	every	sleep
to	him	can	went	good	old
you	is	so	long	don't	call
said	am	them	an	too	let
on	as	would	into	pretty	brown
and	with	could	are	any	by
it	her	see	no	how	after
his	be	like	over	got	help
they	then	me	just	jump	yellow
he	up	when	come	about	their
of	there	not	came	know	well
that	have	one	your	take	make
but	little	will	blue	green	five
a	all	did	it	around	here
in	some	were	ask	right	think
she	go	this	its	where	going
had	down	yes	red	for	six

Group 7	Group 8	Group 9	Group 10	Group 11
walk	tell	soon	use	wash
again	first	has	hurt	live
stop	black	our	sit	upon
cold	goes	warm	under	thank
two	much	made	fast	show
play	try	find	pull	draw
off	white	better	which	these
today	write	ate	read	wish
or	keep	run	say	hot
who	new	only	cut	clean
never	ten	hold	fall	sing
fly	always	full	why	many
before	give	gave	light	because
been	must	us	kind	grow
seven	does	buy	carry	together
myself	drink	those	own	shall
eat	work	open	pick	far
may	start	three	both	best
eight	bring	funny	small	please
round	once	done	found	laugh

Master sheets for the first six groups of the Dolch Words are included in your set of free printables (p.9). Print them out onto card stock and make your own flash cards.

So, now that you know all the first sight words to teach your child, how do you go about doing it? There are many games and activities.

Flash Cards

Flashcards are the old standby, and still an excellent tool. Print out or make up sets on 3x5 index cards, punch a hole in one corner of the cards, and attach them to key rings. The first six groups of Dolch Words shown previously are included for printing onto card stock in your free printables (p.9). When you have a minute anytime, like waiting out a commercial on TV, waiting for dinner, or any other time, go through them until your child knows them well. Here are more flash card resources for you:

Free Dolch Words flash cards and activity ides are at:

www.mrprintables.com/dolch-sight-words.html

Printable Fry words:

www.k12reader.com/subject/sight-words/fry-words

Tablet apps

Tablet apps are a perfect way to learn sight words. Kids love using them, they provide variety and excellent graphics, and your child can use them almost anywhere on a tablet or smartphone. Apps are just about the perfect way to learn to read.

Bitsboard (iPad) has the largest catalog of photos and words available, all in an easy to use format. If you get only one app for sight words, get this one. IMO, this app belongs on every preschooler's iPad.

Sight Words 1-300: Kids Learn (iPad) is another must-have app, with different games to keep things fun and reinforce the sight words.

Fry Words for the iPad has all 1,000 Fry Words. The Android app has 500 Fry Words. The simple, convenient **Sight Words List** (iPad) has sight words grouped by age, but don't let that stop you! Once a young child is in their sensitive period for reading and has progressed to sight words, she can learn them all. You and your child can record you own voices saying the words.

Abby Sight Words (iPad & android) is a really fun app with different activities. Use the lowercase letters option. **My Sight Words** (android) is a good basic sight word reviewer.

The great **Kids Handwriting Grade K** (android) is a nice app that teaches sight words while providing writing practice. Writing words is a great way to remember them.

Compound Words Montessori is a superb app that teaches your child interactively how to combine words to make new words.

<u>Note</u>: Apps like Bitsboard, include words that are not on the basic sight words lists. Introducing these is fine after your child has learned the more basic words on the lists. Common sense dictates that we start with easier words first.

Concentration

The classic 'Concentration' memory game is always fun. Make two cards for each word. Start with, say, 8 words, which makes 16 cards. Shuffle them and lay them out at random, words down, in a 4 X 4 grid pattern. Take turns flipping over two cards at a time and trying to make matches. As you each start to remember where the words are, things will go faster. The player with the most word pairs at the end wins.

Concentration is fun for all ages. Use images and photo cards with younger children. The **Animals Matchup & Memory Game** from Montessori Print Shop is included in your free printables set:

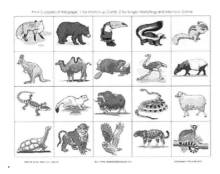

The **Memory King** app (iPad) is good for getting a younger child used to the memory game so he can use it with sight words later on.

Three Part Cards

Montessori Three Part Cards are classic early learning materials. Each card has an illustration or a photo by itself, the name of the object by itself, and the image and the name together:

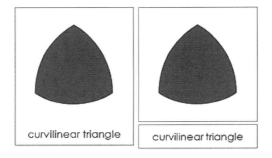

Montessori Print Shop has a huge collection of all kinds of Three Part Cards, as well as clear instructions for their use. The cards can be used to identify and name the objects pictured, learn the names, and match the objects with their names. When your child shows a specific interest in a subject covered by one or more sets of these cards, purchase, download, and print them out for use while your child's interest level is high.

Keep a pack of 3X5 plain index cards and a marker handy. When you come across something interesting or any new word, write it down in block lower case print and add it to your child's sight word collection.

Making Sentences

When your child has learned a good number of sight words, it is time to make sentences and read sentences fluently. As your child learns more sight words, expand his sentence making activities to longer, more complex sentences.

Lay out sight word flash cards, or index cards with sight words written on them in block style lower case letters, at random on a table. The first six groups of Dolch Words shown previously are included for printing onto card stock in your free printables (p.9).

Say a sentence using words your child knows. Have your child find the words and build the sentence. Do many sentences this way. Then, let your child build his own sentences and read them.

| she | has | a | big | boat |

Have your child read each sentence she makes fluently, as if she were talking to someone. Do not worry right now if the first word in the sentences is not capitalized. You can show your child about that as he works on writing. He will also pick this up as you read together.

Most office supply stores sell business card magnets. Write a group of sight words on cards cut to 2 ½ X 3" (business card size) and attach them to the magnets. Put them on your fridge for sight word practice and sentence building when everyone is in the kitchen.

Eureka sight word tiles (above, Amazon) are great for learning words and making sentences.

The **Trend Enterprises Sight Word Bingo Flash Cards** (above, Amazon) are a fun sight word game.

Tablet apps are great for sentence building. **Sentence Maker** (iPad) has great photos, a clean interface, and many customization options. **Sentence Builder** (iPad & android) is a popular sentence app, with two levels and the ability to create your own lessons. **Sentence Magic** (iPad) has two and three word options for children just starting with sight words. **Rainbow Sentences** (iPad) is expensive, but has quite a few customization options and attempts to teach correct grammar by color coding words.

Sight Word Workbooks

Scholastic has an excellent series of sight word workbooks, some for under $10. These are all available on Amazon.

25 Read & Write Mini-Books is a wonderful resource. Your child can make little books, learn sight words, decorate the books, write in words, and then save them to read.

100 Write-And-Learn Sight Word Practice Pages offers sight word recognition, writing practice, sentence building, and reading practice on every page.

40 Sensational Sight Word Games gives your child many entertaining ways to learn sight words. This adds variety and keeps things fresh and interesting. These games will definitely make sight words fun. Keeping things positive and fun is essential.

100 Sight Word Mini-Books provides more experience recognizing words containing common letter combinations. Each mini-book includes a word search game, writing practice, sight word recognition, and reading practice.

Copy pages from these workbooks for repetition. Repeating activities is how children learn.

More sight word resources

Here are more good sight word resources you can download free or for a very reasonable price. Many have wonderful little books so your child can learn sight words the best way possible – by reading them in the context of a sentence in simple books.

Find many sight word activities at this great site:

www.mrsperkins.com/activities.html

These phrases help your child start reading sight words.:

www.mrsperkins.com/phrases.html

Very nice, inexpensive sight word books are available here:

www.sightandsoundreading.com

There are simple, free sight word book printables at:

www.kindergartenkindergarten.com/2011/08/sight-word-readers.html

A printable farm animals sight word book:

www.sightwordsgame.com/wp-content/uploads/2012/01/farm-animals-final.pdf

Work on these sight word activities with your child regularly. Consistent practice will bring the best results.

As your child is moving along with learning sight words, start reading using the first reading books recommended in the next step. From this point on, nothing builds reading skill like reading. You can do all kinds of worksheets, games, and other activities using written language. None will have the lasting positive effects on a child's reading ability of simply reading. Find books at your child's level and read, read, read. When your child is ready, provide slightly more challenging books to read.

Learning sight words by writing

Writing is one of the best ways to remember information, including sight words. Have pads of blank practice writing sheets always available for practice writing of sight words.

There are excellent sites online where you can create, save, and print your own writing practice sheets, customized to your child's specific needs. Create and print out sheets with sight words your child is currently working on, sentences made using these and other sight words, your child's name, and other words. Here are a few of these sites:

www.worksheetworks.com/english/writing/handwriting.html

tools.atozteacherstuff.com/printable-handwriting-practice-worksheet-maker

www.handwritingforkids.com/handwrite/manuscript/texts/14words-index.php

Step Three: Reading!

Shutterstock

The next step is to keep on reading with your child every day while you also encourage him to read independently. As she learns more and more sight words, and reads familiar books more than once, your child will start to read more on her own. Encourage and support this process while also reading aloud every day. Here are specific steps you can take to help:

- Make a daily reading time (or two) a regular part of your child's day. Take this time to read yourself.

- Whenever your child feels that he can read even one sentence or phrase, let him.

- When he has trouble reading a word, tell him what it is and move on.

- Encourage fluent, conversational reading (p.74-75) rather than reading one-word-at-a-time. If your child stops to figure out a word or learn a new one, encourage him to read the entire sentence again fluently, as if speaking to someone.

- Avoid following along under words with your finger, and encourage your child not to.

- If you and your child like to watch TV, turn on the close captioning and help your child as needed to read the captions.

- Read the books your child is most interested in. Let your child pick books out. Keep looking for new, high interest reading material while your child is reading current favorites. Help your child make her own books (p.93) based on her experiences.

Good first reading books

When your child is ready to move into first reading books, here are suggestions:

Kipper's A to Z: An Alphabet Adventure

The Icky Bug Alphabet Book

Eating the Alphabet

Brown Bear, Brown Bear, What Do You See?

Bubble Trouble

You Read To Me, I'll Read To You: Very Short Stories To Read Together

Good Luck Bear

Thank you Bear

Why Mosquitoes Buzz In People's Ears

Where's Spot

Spot's First Words

Rosie's Walk

Spot Goes To School

Have You Seen My Cat?

My Mother Is Mine

Goodnight Dog

Hop On Pop

Green Eggs and Ham

Are You My Mother?

The Cat In The Hat

Horton Hears a Who

How the Grinch Stole Christmas

The Snowy Day

Alexander and the Terrible, Horrible, No Good Very Bad Day

The Rose In My Garden

Blueberries For Sal

The Napping House

All The World

My Garden

The Giving Tree

The Big Dipper

** This is one of the wonderful "Lets Read and Find Out" Science series

Boo Hoo Bird

Bringing the Rain to Kapiti Plain

Terrific

At Night

Every Friday

One is a Snail, Ten is a Crab: A Counting by Feet Book

Where the Wild Things Are

The 'How Do Dinosaurs' series

Today and Today

Curious George

Leo The Late Bloomer

Gregory, The Terrible Eater

The Day Jimmy's Boa Ate The Wash

The Ball Bounced

Animals Should Definitely Not Wear Clothing

The Jacket I Wear In the Snow

Drummer Hoff

Hattie and the Fox

The I Can Read Leveled Readers **(www.icanread.com/index.cfm)** are a great resource. Find individual titles, starting with the Shared Reading series, and search them on Amazon or Barnes & Noble. They may also be in your local bookstore. Many of their readers have Kindle editions. These make good starting books for you to read with your child at this stage.

eBooks

The Fantastic Flying Books of Mr. Morris Lessmore

There are many good eBooks and collections for the iPad and android tablets. eBooks take reading to a new level by including interactive features, the option to have the book read to you as well as to read it yourself, games and other in-app fun like artwork and puzzles, and many other elements. Some eBooks make more use of these than others; but the trend is to higher quality eBooks all the time. One day, our children will look at paper books as curious relics!

Interactive eBooks
Reviewing the latest Interactive eBooks

New high quality eBooks and interactive eBooks are coming all the time, so keep up on Scholastic's wonderful **Storia eBooks** site, and on **Interactive eBooks**. You can search the Amazon Kindle store for top rated children's books, and also check out **bestappsforkids.com**, where they review and rate apps, books, and more. **Kindoma** (iPad) offers a collection of nice children's eBooks.

Here are examples of good eBooks and eBook collections for early readers for the iPad and for Android devices:

iPad eBooks

Bookboard

Dr. Seuss Beginner Book Collection #1

MeeGenius! Kid's Books

Kindoma

14 Best of the Best preschooler's books for iPad

Booksy Learn To Read Books

Scholastic eBooks

The Oceanhouse Media Collection Check out the Magic School Bus eBooks

Disney Digital Books

Bartelby's Book of Buttons (Vol. 1 & 2)

Good Night Moon

Rounds: Parker Penguin

Rounds: Franklin Frog

The Chalk Box Story

Sleepy Mole's Moving Day

Five Little Monkeys Jumping On The Bed

How Rocket Learned to Read

Bella Goes Bump In The Night

Mouse and Owl Check out School Zone's Start To Read! Series

Go Clifford, Go!

I Love You Through and Through

Finding Nemo: My Puzzle Book

Pop Out! The Tale of Peter Rabbit

The Three Little Pigs by Nosy Crow

Cinderella

The Penguins of Madagascar: Read & Play

Hiding Hannah

Android eBooks

Dr. Seuss Books (Google Play)

Dr. Seuss Books (Amazon)

Oceanhouse Media Books

Booksy Learn To Read Platform

MeeGenius! Children's Books

iStoryBooks

Read Me Stories

Just Grandma and Me

Good Night Moon

The Going to Bed Book

Ant and Grasshopper 3D

Good Night Train

The Grumpy Family

Grandpa Grumpy's Family

There are many sites for free and inexpensive children's eBooks. At Barnes & Noble (**www.barnesandnoble.com**), click 'Kids' and 'Online Storytime'.

At **www.magickeys.com/books**, you will find a large collection of storybooks your child can read online.

Search **www.techsupportalert.com/free-books-children** for free online eBooks.

Improving Comprehension

Learning to read is great, but it is just the beginning. Your child needs to remember and understand what she reads. This is reading comprehension, a vital skill. Without comprehension, reading is just a mechanical decoding process that does not stimulate your child to think. Reading comprehension, like all skills, is developed through practice. Luckily, this is easy to do at home.

Reading comprehension is improved by *talking* about books before, during, and after they are read. You don't need special workbooks or programs for this.

Before you and your child read a book, talk about it. If it is one you've read before, what does your child remember about it? Who are the characters? What happens to them? If it is a new book, what does your child think it might be about? Flip through the pages before you read the book and get your child's ideas. Stimulate thinking about the book.

During the reading, ask your child what she thinks will happen next, and what she thinks about what is happening. Does he remember the story from reading the book before? Is the book making her feel something - scared, anxious, happy, or curious? Who are her favorite characters and why? Does she like the story or not? How would she change the story if she could?

After reading, talk about what happened in the story. Ask your child questions about the characters - what did they say, what did they do, who are her most and least favorite characters and why? Talk about the meaning of the story and how it might relate to your child's life. Doe he agree with what the characters did? What would he tell someone else if they asked what the story was about?

All this discussion will get your child thinking and paying attention when she reads, which is the key to comprehension. Here are more tips for improving comprehension:

- Read every day.

- Repeat reading favorite books. Talk about the book each time to assess what your child remembers.

- Have your child reread passages aloud. Encourage fluency.

- Connect what your child is reading with her life experiences. *"Who does that remind you of?" "What did we do last week that was like this?" "Does this make you think of anyone in our family?"*

- Concentrate on specific paragraphs or pages and talk about what is being presented.

- Encourage your child to draw or paint something inspired by the book.

- Make flashcards with any new words encountered while reading. Talk about the meaning of each word and practice sight word recognition and defining words using these flash cards.

- Talk about different aspects of the story, like the setting, characters, plot, and the outcome.

- Find books that also have been made into movies and watch the videos as well as reading the book. Compare the book with the movie.

- Provide a wide variety of reading material, including books, eBooks, magazines, postcards, etc.

"A child does not read until he receives ideas from the written word."

Maria Montessori

Making your own books

Young children learn to read much faster and easier if they are highly interested in what they are reading about. What could be more interesting than a child's own life? Almost everything your child does and experiences, even dreams, can provide the subject matter for homemade books. A book your child makes that talks about her life experiences or comes from her own imagination is almost guaranteed to be high interest material.

A bookmaking project at The Artistic Life

Homemade books are not hard to create. Keep supplies on hand, like glue sticks, computer printer, plain white paper, and a stapler. Put a sheet of colored construction paper on top of a few sheets of white paper, fold in half, staple along the fold, and you have a book. You can also punch holes in two card stock sheets for the covers and along one side of the pages and tie the book together with yarn.

When your child has an interesting experience, idea, or dream, ask him if he would like to make a book about it. Let your child illustrate her book with her own drawings, photos you print out, pictures from magazines, etc. If he is not writing well enough to write on his own, have him dictate what each page should say. Help him tell the story as needed, but only if he gets stuck. This is your child's book. There is a nice blog post on making books at:

www.teachpreschool.org/2010/02/making-books-with-children

Tips for making books at home:

- Keep it simple, neat, and organized. Children care much less about fancy crafts projects than adults.

- Let your child choose her words. Talk about the story or topic and make all the suggestions you like, but let your child come up with the words for the books on her own, then use her words.

- Show your child how to structure each book with a cover and title, perhaps a table of contents and a dedication page, the body of the book, and an ending.

- If you want to get creative, try different bindings. Yarn, ribbons, colored tape, clip rings – there are many ways besides stapling.

- If your child tires of the project, stop or take a break, but pick it up again another time until the book is finished. This teaches a child to bring projects to a conclusion.

At **lovelydesign.blogspot.com**, type 'homemade children's books' in the search box to find instructions for making cute little books (photo above).

When your child is writing, she can write the text for her books herself. Until then, have her dictate what to write and write it in yourself using block letters, like the style the sandpaper letters are made in. If you do the text on a computer, use Century Gothic or a similar type, as used in the sandpaper letters earlier. Homemade books are wonderful early readers, precious memories, and great gifts to give to loved ones.

There are great apps for making your own eBooks. Some make it easy to add photos, share your child's books, and take advantage of all the techno-tools. **Scribblepress** (iPad) allows your child to create all kinds of eBooks. Your child can add photos or illustrations, and use stock images and templates. **My Story** (iPad) is another great children's book creation app. Books can include recordings, and can be shared with others, even published to the iBookStore. **Book Press** (iPad) is a free keepsake bookmaking app that many people love. **Story Patch** (iPad) has many options for story templates, creating new stories, and other features.

Encouraging reading

Reading has a lot of competition for a child's attention these days! Children are becoming accustomed to 'show me' style learning, with videos on almost any topic. Reading is often essential for using other forms of media, but many children today spend less time reading entire books. What can you do to encourage your child to read? What if your child dislikes or hates reading?

First, cover the basics. Are you and your spouse setting good examples by reading every day? Are you reading with your child every day? Be sure that reading is practiced, valued, and encouraged in your home and family. Are you providing books your child is highly interested in or has chosen herself? Have your tried making your own books (p.93)? Did you rush through the phonics and sight word steps? These skills require quite a bit of practice for children to achieve real mastery.

Here are more ideas:

- Read every day. Read aloud to your child and have her read also.

- Be a good reading role model.

- Teach your child songs and rhymes. Type them up and have your child read the words.

- Turn on the closed captioning on your child's favorite tv shows.

- Pair books with unabridged audio books.

- Have your child write a little every day.

- Have your child read passages into a recording device or a tablet app for voice recording and listen to herself.

- Avoid nagging, bribing, judging, and criticizing.

- Observe for anything that sparks your child's interest and find or make appropriate reading material about it.

- Give your child a book allowance and buy subscriptions to favorite magazines.

- Ask your child to read you a story.

- Take your child to the library often.

- Ask your child to help you read to accomplish tasks, like reading ingredients on food labels, looking for the right aisle in the store, reading traffic signs, etc.

- Set aside a special place for your child's books. Provide supplies for simple bookmaking there.

- Play games that involve reading.

- Allow your child to stay up 15-20 minutes late at night if she uses the time to read.

- Make a chart or graph that show how many books your child has read.

Parting Note

Thank you for bringing this book into your home. I hope the materials and activities shown and linked here help you give your child the lifelong gift of reading. Early readers tend to do better in school, especially at first when building confidence is so important. Good reading and comprehension skills are essential in today's world, where more people than ever are constantly in touch; but people are losing their interest in reading. Helping your child develop a love for reading in the early years is an opportunity easily missed.

If doing reading activities proves to be fun, I encourage you to check out math, science, art, music, geography, and culture materials and activities for little ones. Whatever you put in front of those absorbent minds goes right in!

About the author

John Bowman's most rewarding career was being a Montessori preschool Teacher and center Director. His goals now are to encourage parents to do early learning activities with their children, and to show them how.